birth chart

For Mama Elaine,
a poet herself,
+ the ultimate Leo.
Love,
Rachel

"I am Ginger writing this
                    poem
and if you don't like it
        send me home"

XO♥ + lots of love

birth chart

rachel feder

![ee] excelsior **editions**

AN IMPRINT OF STATE UNIVERSITY OF NEW YORK PRESS

Published by State University of New York Press, Albany
© 2020 State University of New York Press

Excelsior Editions is an imprint of State University of New York Press

For information, contact State University of New York Press, Albany, NY
www.sunypress.edu

Library of Congress Cataloging-in-Publication Data

Names: Feder, Rachel, author.
Title: Birth chart / Rachel Feder.
Description: Albany : Excelsior Editions, an imprint of State University of New York
    Press, [2020] | Includes bibliographical references.
Identifiers: LCCN 2019032773 | ISBN 9781438479361 (paperback) | ISBN
    9781438479378 (ebook)
Subjects: LCSH: Birth charts—Poetry. | Astrology and childbirth—Poetry.
Classification: LCC PS3606.E333 A6 2020 | DDC 811/.6—dc23
LC record available at https://lccn.loc.gov/2019032773

10 9 8 7 6 5 4 3 2 1

For my scorpions

contents

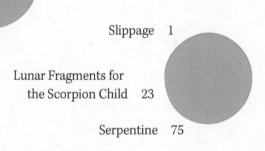

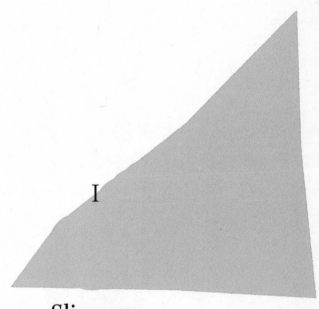

I

Slippage

It's almost the year of the earth pig, thank God   because my kid has stomach flu

      & we need a fresh start   Cleaning the carpet   my husband said

we have to move   & Nan said *I love the Chinese almanac: here are the days to fuck*

      someone, here are the days to avoid trolleys, here are the types of people

you need to suck up to,   here are the days to wear red underwear. NO

      BULLSHIT keep your ear to the ground or pulse to the nose or whatever   that last one

being a wrong idiom the way she once wrote

                            bread and potatoes of the immigrant experience

      & I wrote *carb hound!*   But being golden, we love the moon & the lunar year's

dark ascent   & slow revelations   & I said *Shit*

now I need to add another problematic poem to my book as the scorpion child raced

                     across the loft holding a light bulb   and I shouted

NO   to keep him from dropping it over

the banister   & when he cried I told him   *my "mean voice" is my gift to keep you safe*

but I couldn't tell him who gave it to me   & ended up saying *God*   & *Mother*

Nature & *the Universe* & explaining too much about light bulbs

     how they work & of what   they are made & what might happen   I said too much about illumination

about the world in fragments

last night Nan took her son to the hospital

because we've always been yoked together

& her daughter fed the cats including the cats of others who needed feeding

& I said *send me that fire pig energy* & regarding this book & its celestial disarray

she said *I will take responsibility for any cultural misappropriations you can say that*

in your acknowledgments It's always a good day

to avoid trolleys it's never a good day to move a Taurus manifesto

Over shishito peppers, Rebecca & I discuss H.D. & matrilineal descent. Our conversation turns the room red because I'm the useless kind of synesthete. I tell her she is basically a Scorpio which is a lot for her to process because she's basically a Scorpio. The other Rebecca in my life, not Daphne du Maurier's *Rebecca* which I am saving and don't you spoil it, is a Pisces moon, & when I told her this she said *yes but Barnum effect and all that* which is such a fishy way of accepting a compliment. H.D. had friends too, her friend Silvia Dobson, her dragon, wrote her a letter about shopping for goldfish. Rebecca means *servant of God.* In the letter, Silvia Dobson calls H.D. *My dear cat* & writes, *I rang boldly and entered a new world. Fish Enthusiasts are new to me.* I write a letter to the state of Massachusetts asking for Robert Lowell's birth certificate because somewhere outside Woodstock the scorpion child demands *Yellow Submarine* on repeat while the road undulates beneath me and I think *I myself am hell; / nobody's here—*. My husband asks which of my most-hated songs I would rather have on a desert island (he's a Virgo sun), *Yellow Submarine* or *Don't You Want Me* by The Human League, convinced the utopian vision of the former (which, excuse me sir, is profoundly *dys*topian) would be the better island jam, at least at first, although he admits *Don't You Want Me* would remind one that sometimes it's better to be alone and I say *how can you know me all these years and not realize that* Don't You Want Me, *while among the worst of all possible songs, is profoundly and extremely the ideal desert island song insofar as it's a mopey ballad you can dance to, thereby providing both catharsis and cardiovascular exercise?* If he were on a desert island he'd build something, write a message in a bottle, I'd be eating fruit in the trees. Only civilization could have brought us together. Only civilization and the comet in his chest. Once, regarding a romper she was wearing in Brooklyn, Rebecca, definitely the Pisces moon one, said *it's like am I wearing this because I actually think it's cool or because its presumption of coolness somehow flickers back & forth from presumption to actuality moment to moment?* She sends me Barthes on astrology: *the stars insistently and wisely prescribe more sleep, always more.* I know the house burns down but I don't know if he did it. She corrects me, *I always thought Rebecca meant* ensnarer.

The fish salesman *might have been Aquarious himself* and might have been a conman. The dragon reports to her cat that *Golden gold-fish are almost too expensive to buy but you can get brown ones which colour up during the summer. If there is much sun and warmth, they colour quickly. If the weather is bad, they may not glitter till Autumn time.* I am waiting for a letter from the state of Massachusetts that says *Robert Lowell was a Pisces what else do you need to know*? Chet, a Gemini, says *either you only live this life once or else you live this life over and over and either way you want that cake.* The dragon says this *seemed like a little fable.* Rebecca has the moon, Venus, Mars, and Uranus in Scorpio, not to mention Scorpio rising, which is why she identifies with both H.D. and Antigone. My husband has the moon, Mars, and Uranus in Scorpio, not to mention Scorpio rising, which is why he could survive for a long time in the jungle. Writing to her friend about her fishpond, Silvia Dobson explains, *Today I planted up the pool but the fish must not go in for a fortnight. You won't get sparkling clear water for a twelve-month, said Aquarius. Don't on any account try to clear the green away for it will get thicker and thicker and then, at the right moment, come like crystal.* The dragon hunts for fishes on a *narrow sordid street* in a *stark bombed area.* My great-grandfather, one of twelve, was the only sibling to make it across the Atlantic, but I have forgotten the story as I've forgotten the language. En route to Paris I spun Natalie Merchant's *Tigerlily* in my Discman, eager to meet lost cousins who would complain about their soft stomachs, spurring an instantaneous feeling of kinship. In *The Gift*, H.D. writes, *A child born under a star? But that didn't mean anything. Why, every child was born under a star.* The neighbors set off firecrackers as a shadow creeps across the moon. *They say I must be one of the wonders of God's own creation.* All these years later, orange and green are still my favorite colors, the way they came together on the cover, & I would happily live on unpasteurized cheese. The scorpion child says *my imagination is just about fire.* Earth's shadow reddens the moon, confusing fish & scorpions. Natalie Merchant is a Scorpio, too.

Waxing crescent moon in Sagittarius
                            & what the fuck
                            do I want
                            to manifest
beyond stilling time, its slippage

In the scorpion queen group text, the scorpion queens are talking

                about their vaginas.

They say we are making shit happen the way Latour says

                 things happen.

I am not a scorpion but an interloper, always

                  in the pit

on the desert floor, they are telling me to bill the patriarchy, they are telling me

get on a train, go somewhere, go to Philadelphia, the Lake District

  we agree if men got IUDs but   I you don't   we agree

on the dragon as suggestive emoji holding   that crystal wrapping around

Bruno Latour, fire pig, lion moon, classic fucking Gemini

  Venus, Uranus, and the sun in Gemini

hence all that pushback against subjects vs. objects actors! networks! Dragons!

You guys

     your vaginas are perfect how could they not be perfect

but it's never OK to disagree with a scorpion not even

   about her own perfection

as we slide on into that station

   where we have always

been modern

Waxing crescent moon in Sagittarius   a million stock photos of the moon

the birds flying

by the morning   moon

I wish Aquarius would get born before we perish.

When I call myself a sleeping bear the scorpion
child says *& I'm the cub with you*
   a better lesson
   than all Aesop's fables combined

bear mother, dragon mother
reclined in the chair at her childhood
   dentist, where they still play
   Dave Matthews & call her

young lady! At the park the scorpion
decides crashing is the new breaking
   which is not not a statement
   of praxis & into me he is

or someday was a Capricorn, obviously,
like a swimming goat, Dave Matthews
   I mean, a grass fire on the hill
   and the way the light came

through the window, when I was
young, once, a lady, I guess, in a manner
   of speaking, my purple notebook
   my own alma mater

My Virgo ascendant wants to buy a house.

My Taurus sun wants to upgrade the furniture.

My Gemini moon   forgot to tell me what she wants   she's too busy

    rubbing the snake oil into her legs

        and winding down the staircase

    her mind buzzing

        like her mind

According to Emily aka *The Voluptuous Witch* Jupiter is a sugar daddy & when he's in
      Sagittarius it's time for me to work some house magic

and I do, lugging a desk upstairs & hanging the *ketubah* emblazoned with a watercolor
      pomegranate, plump sign of futurity.

At the Eastman Museum, I start getting snappy.
      There's a fake elephant head where a real elephant head once hung

reminding me that photography has its genesis in that concentrated iris which
      I mean   that confiscated iris   I

In the dragon stories, the dragon always has a den, I always make it cozy.
The scorpion child turns on the fire to *make it be cozy.*

The pomegranate is a sign of fertility.

If I wanted a tattoo, which I don't, I'd carve it
      on my wrist.

I left Colorado for western New York just to see the Maroon Bells on a box of tissues

      George Eastman was a Cancer & no offense to my Cancer girls (including the one
who painted the pomegranate) but that explains his perverse sense that an elephant

      would be best enjoyed at home just
give me a moment   inside the camera obscura   its heavy-ass curtain
                                     falling
to reveal the image of the garden   something in the eyes   the elephant's eyes

      gave it away   their marble unreality   upside-down image

silver chloride   quicksilver   a school of fish scattering   as the elephant steps

     into the water

                       I think I broke my eye inside the camera obscura,
                       all that concentrated light.

The moon follows the car says the scorpion child & not to be that horse girl
from the '90s but I put on a song by the Dave Matthews Band & ask him to
listen for just that lyric & then I start to recognize bits and pieces of stories
I think I can I think I can and I realize this has always been a song for a child,
which explains why I loved it when I was a child.

In the scorpion queen group text, the scorpion queens are discussing

their camera rolls, scrolling

fast past portraits

of their mutinous vaginas. They are doing this at the Museum of the Word, making

passersby blush

like chimeras.   This is a euphemism for exegesis, like

the vagina itself.   The scorpion queens are startled to find seven photographs

of a Gemini husband,

indivisible by two   emerging, dripping wet, from the shower.

A towel at once obfuscates his corporeal form and renders

the photographs more intimate

as captured by a Pisces child   her tiny wild heart   Mercury & Venus in Aquarius

fish in the water as in the trees   climbing   and I am trying

to say something about form // Platonic ideals // & drier modes of inquiry

but the message escapes me   because the medium is too fucking pure, man.

Standing in the kitchen, my husband says *I'm glad this has brought you*
some joy, which is the most Virgo response possible.
Upstairs, the child lies flat on the table of my back
the way scorpion babies ride on their mamas.

I dreamt u sent me a parrot & I thought *what is this statement of praxis?*

There is no dragon in this poem, unless
the dragon is Form itself.

Jack Kerouac
was a Pisces.
What
the fuck
is a Pisces

The moon waxes toward Purim & Mercury

      goes retrograde which means   it is not going backward

but appears to be going backward   I tell the children the story of Esther

      a queen who revealed the hidden parts of herself

which is why we wear masks   we hide our faces to celebrate revelation

      it's a twisted logic   you thought the Victorian frog who bows & bears

a bouquet was *not the enemy but rather the objective correlative*

                                      of our contempt for the enemy

              thus revealing your secret kindness/thus revealing that I am awful

     & Nan tells us the scorpion child's dreams are auspicious

even when they wake him at 3am which Matchbox Twenty promised would be lonely

     & he won't go back to sleep because a dragon is there.

Jeremy Fisher is an illuminated manuscript   the source text is an amulet

     also known as Beatrix Potter's brass

frog doorstop, which she brought to life

                                      her lover died though

When it starts raining in the kitchen Nan says

                              Confucius says small water disasters in spring

     bring good luck & when I say *you made that up* she says *just the Confucius part*

but Confucius is a construct   on the first day of spring a car taps your child so gently

     if it were anything else   a bee   a brush from a stranger

but you cry in your office, your Aquarius moon reminded of its, our

     precarity. Esther didn't ask to be queen she was only tending her garden.

Didn't ask to be anything.   The child applies glue, presses sequins

to a paper mask. We fold *hamantaschen* dough into fertility cookies seeded and fruitful.

I asked *is the water still fortuitous*
     if it's from a malfunctioning toilet & Nan said *let me consult the books of the ancients.*

Days ago you sent us photographs from Lake Elsinore, all poppies & painted ladies.

                    Orange, a color named after a fruit.

I said *auspicious nightmares & toilets 4 realz?*

     & she said *for realz but you still have to take care of business you know you still have to be a woman & hold the bag.*

Teach me about dragons, or don't.
The language of explanation is a heart emoji.
It means you know what I mean.

The scorpion children play dragon and unicorn,
by which I mean   they play with fire.

They were born one day apart
        and that is the day that always seems to be between them,   wide open.

The night of the super blood wolf moon I maybe hurt
my teeth on some overcooked potatoes. I read
Where the Wild Things Are, lining up the moon
on the page with the moon in the window, whispering
my same wild song as the scorpion child falls asleep
with his leg against my shoulder. I am the place
where someone loves you best of all. The wolf part
of the wolf moon refers to the hungry beasts of January
though the woman who cut my hair told me it refers to *pack*
energy, or maybe that's the same thing. She has two tattoos
of the moon, one for the moon under which each child was born. We were born
under waxing crescents, we are just getting started honey, we are just getting started.

II

Lunar

Fragments

for the

Scorpion Child

This is a lunar fragment
       for the scorpion child
             who will not sleep, the stripes of his pajama shirt
                     against the dinosaurs of his pajama pants, the bonnie
            he calls bunny who lies over the ocean, oh bring back
      my bunny to me, oh
lie down, scorpion child

☾

I had a strange Yom Kippur
          insofar as I did not fast
insofar as I reread Jamaica Kincaid's *Lucy*
          while the child slept on
me last time I read *Lucy* I shared a tent
          with Chet by the snake
preserve, snakes on the desert floor
          and in glass terrariums,
this was before we met our husbands.
          Today a bee flew into my hair and became tangled in my half-knot, my
scorpion mother pulled it out with her hands and was, unsurprisingly, stung.

I don't know what happened to the bee.

The first time I read *Lucy* I couldn't get over her mother's letters,
          how she hoards them in her room and won't open them and won't
read them, even the letter marked *urgent*. It occurs to me that I am fundamentally
          a person who opens letters

and apologizes, which Lucy never seems to do, which is what Yom Kippur is for, or is
supposed to be for, not that I spent it apologizing.

The day broke into night and the moon hung by halves and the scorpion child clutched
my shoulders as if frightened by the brightness of the stars. I know even before I look it
up that Jamaica Kincaid is a Gemini. My moon is in Gemini

but I'm still learning what that means

☾

At the Vermeer exhibit

        the scorpion child called every lute

a *guitar* a white-haired woman

        pointed at him and said *I want you to remember this when you're 15!*

I wanted to say

    he really doesn't

have to that's not how

      art works I wanted to shout   *Vermeer was a Scorpio too* you can tell

by the skin which always seems to be

        on fire at air & space there are three stones

from the moon that I want to put in the poem without explanation

    the way you could hide them in a neighbor's garden and nobody would notice

basalt and we stood among the butterflies *anorthosite* where a pink-spotted cattleheart

refused   to give up her Taurean secrets (*typical*) & a morpho perched on us both

at the same time   for a moment

        for some brave and stupid reason you let the volunteer convince you

to touch the Madagascar hissing cockroach hold the caterpillar hopper stick insect

the moon waxed from Pisces into Aries   *breccia* which means nothing to me

☾

The scorpion child says his *favorite animal is the moon,*

then laughs   & says *giraffe.*   The moon

is exalted in Jackson Pollock's chart. I said   *I could do that*   & my scorpion mother

said *but you didn't*   & it's super true,   I didn't

so   *mazel tov*   Aquarius king &
                    happy 106ᵗʰ today   theoretically   you could have

made it to the   party.

The color orange extremely is a Gemini.

The color orange is talking to you.   My Gemini moon

a harvest moon   rises like a clementine.   It rises

oh my darling   like an animal

☾

The night of the mid-autumn festival Alex Dimitrov tweets *the moon can get it* & I think
       yes that is poetry but when I try to write a moon poem it's all *the moon,*
like everything else, is a continuous cycle of desire & then like something something
              the irregularities of ovulation that night
is both Sukkot & Chinese Thanksgiving and Nan says her mom
       says *any time there's a super round moon you are the fullest*
              version of who you are and the mid-autumn moon is the roundest
she also says *don't eat anything that's not round 'cause you fuck shit up if you do*
& my son says the moon *says nighttime, it says nighttime.*
       I have no harvest but turn
the cut bowl of the pomegranate upside-
       down in my hand and smack it with a wooden spoon,
loosening the seeds and the scorpion child (*it says nighttime*) gives me that look
       that says while he knows my wisdom is limited, it is also infinite
Fuck I ate a bunch of French fries, I reply and when Nan
       says *used to be round* I realize I am, fundamentally, a person
who justifies eating French fries because they used to be round//

When the scorpion child wants help, he says *let me help you.*

In spite of nothing, when he won the Nobel Prize,
              Albert Camus's first thought was of his mother.

Let's not break it. Let's get ready for the beautiful day.

☾

On *shemini atzeret*

        in the Target parking lot

            the paper cut moon

                    surprises me & when the scorpion child

          looks up he says *it's too bright*

          which comes out

as *bite*   *bite*   *bite*

☾

The moon is in Taurus

                     & the morning after, the child
wakes up an actual scorpion, Kafkaesque
but cuter, and would you have burned
      his manuscripts if you
           had been the friend Kafka asked
to do so, when he died? I know
      I couldn't have and couldn't
Kafka was a Cancer, which explains everything
      like why didn't he do it himself,
or if OK he can't do it now,
      why didn't he do it earlier, like
why did he wait, & if he means it
      why ask me, the girl least likely
                (let's be real) of his acquaintance
      to follow through on something
like this? In graduate school
      they taught us *burn your own notebooks*
I said *even the purple one* they said *even the purple one.*
      I swear on a soft-shell
crab this happened. The scorpion
      refers to his own happiness
using both the long and short forms
      of his name.

〖

On Nan's birthday I kept trying to write a poem like *here is a visitation*

for the scorpion queen

but the moon was waning all day in Libra and like

what

is Libra the thing about Nan which is also the thing about me

is we were   both born under the new moon which explains why slash how

we write in the dark and can only read each other, the lines

opening up and into an unknowing which is its own way of saying nothing

writing is a lie that tells the truth   or something

Nan does it even surprise you at all that Walter "Walt" Whitman was a Gemini?

Sometimes I can't get away from that guy.

we were both born in the year of the ox and everyone in your life is a Taurus

especially me

☾

I am skimming the edges of Turner's watercolors, which are my favorite song.

I am spending too long in a small exhibition.

I am looking for the sea monsters and falling in love with orange.

I am buying new bowls and plates, all orange.

I am reading a commonplace book beside the easel.

I am *Rachel* in the sentence *and there's the Turner, and there's Rachel.*

I am peering at the hills from a corner window.

I am talking about *Ullswater, Cumberland* (1835), which John Ruskin called

the most perfect peace.

I am graphite and watercolor on paper.

I am, like Joseph Mallord William Turner, a Taurus.

We nestle our horns together in the morning fog.

We produce more than we consume and consume more than we should.

We rise early or sometimes terribly late.

We add honey and coconut milk to the coffee and write a poem in declaratives

while the scorpion child sleeps in our bed, his forehead burning,

while a distant train lets its whistle slide through the cold air.

☾

Four centuries ago this month,

Galileo discovered Ganymede,

the third moon of Jupiter

or rather his Sagittarius moon   discovered the moon,

which is such a Sagittarius moon thing to do,   being comforted,   as it is,

by notions   of expansion.   Jasper   is new but

you can see it already   in his clenched fists   & wide open eyes   & longing

to discover.   The scorpion child

has the moon in Sagittarius too,   but if the moon   links us   to our moment

of birth, then what does this say   about me?   Galileo

at least   lived up   to his moon.   Ganymede

is made up of metallic iron,   rock,   and ice.   I too   have a complex

geological history.   A mother   is the largest satellite   in any given

solar system.   Ganymede   disguised as an eagle   traveled to Olympus

& became the cup-bearer for the gods.   You looked a great horned owl in its yellow eyes   the way I look in your eyes   when I bring you milk

at night.   Bright dark rays surround   phantom craters   we call

palimpsests

☾

I want to put the arctic air to bed.
I want to tuck it in among the ice,

                                       read it a story about a train
who is afraid. I want to tell the arctic air
                                              the monster is really a hedgehog.

This morning, Niagara Falls is frozen and the arctic air is crying out for *mama*
        and I'm inside, touching the scorpion child's forehead
first with my hand, then with my lips,   waiting

        for his fever to thaw

☾

Sheera's moon is in Libra
      unless she's getting her time of birth wrong
which is totally possible. This explains
      why she tries to be everything
to everyone as in the 1997 jam
      by alternative rock band Everclear,
and why she blanched
      when Nan brought up menstruation
in a course on Jane Eyre (Scorpio AF)

      I am always breaking
          my resolution
              to clean the red room.

I am always breaking
      my resolution
to sweep under the moors. Charlotte Brontë
          was a Taurus
which explains the invention of Emily (such a Leo) as well as of Jane herself,
      who I always thought was a Virgo but who is really a fucking Leo
                        when you think about it.

My New Year's resolution is to organize my lions.

Yeah, you do   what you do.

      You say what you say.

☾

Astrology reconciles the sky at any given moment with the sky at the moment of your birth such that anything you do—peel an egg, say, or an orange, if you'd rather—corresponds, both with celestial bodies, and with the maternal body in pain.

Regarding a pony that glows in the dark, my child's friend tells me *she's only for the nighttime.*

In the morning, my child tells me *it's blue again,* meaning the sky. Come evening, resisting bedtime, he tells me *it's blue again a little more.*

The morning of the full moon in Sagittarius I wake up early and the house is a disaster, the scorpion child finally asleep after the long durée of bedtime, his father in jeans and unbrushed teeth beside him and me, *just me,* as he says, with two books about mice open on my chest although last night he told me, *no mouses.*

Thus the Brussels sprouts left out and the orange ball of Play-Doh coming to an insistent crust, the way orange snow fell in Europe, tinted by Saharan dust.

Regarding the moon, Chani Nicholas says *Sag is a big feeling and the full moon is also a big feeling.*

The scorpion child says *mommy, something is wrong with me,* by which he means he's tired. He says, *I'm hungry* when he isn't; he's just tired.

☽

I want to write a confessional poem but my biggest confession is that Sylvia Plath

gets into my shoulders. Just thinking about her gives me a weird feeling

in my shoulders like what are they doing just hanging out there

under my neck ugh   This means I can't read her at night, not

that I don't love her

after all I tend to love Scorpios,

not to mention Libra moons,

the conjunction of which explains

the confessional mode, by which I mean a passionate intensity

that has to *explain*, that cares   what you think or (let's be real) feel.

I have cancelled our plans on account of the inclement weather.

I have cancelled our plans
                              on account of the ice storm, on account

of the fact of thaw

☾

my love's an asteroid

        and what if it hits something?

            when I say *I*, you say *you*

                when I say *I*, the scorpion child says *love you.*

            when my scorpion mother sings

            always have to steal my kisses from,

he croons, *you, you, you, you,*   *you*

☾

Scorpions hide from the full moon   especially in Sagittarius
          technically the full moon is this morning   technically the full moon is invisible
technically my Gemini moon doesn't believe in technology
          technically I should be grading a stack of papers about *1984*
instead of writing a slight poem about the technicalities   of the moon
          Orwell's moon, like his sun, was in Cancer   and he had Neptune
in Cancer   and Mercury and Pluto   if Pluto is a thing   in Gemini
          whereas Kafka   yes   *that* Kafka   had his sun and Jupiter
in Cancer   and then in Gemini he had
          the moon, Mercury, Venus, Saturn, Pluto,   again caveats   about Pluto
                                                                                                          and Chiron
of which I have not heard   but anyway   that explains all the bugs
                                                                                        and all the bugging

☾

The sun is a bomb cyclone

                                         the sun is frigid, a ball of bitter fire

in *the trances of the blast*, a sphere of frostbit plasma & frozen hydrogen

punishing neon shiver of

                                       strange and extreme silentness

low-burnt fire / quivers not / all the hot   Coleridge watches the frost crawl across

the window but guys he's holding a baby / the scorpion child peels a banana, eats
      the banana, says the peel is *like a spider*

Like a spider, Coleridge's moon was in Cancer

                where it was comfortable, where it was powerful, where it was freezing

this explains his mood swings and extreme attachments if not everything
                            & yes I mean everything

                                        quietly shining to the quiet moon

☾

A child makes a zoographia of open things.

        An empty banana peel is a *spider*. His hand underwater is a *little*

                    octopus. The infant earth

got slammed by Theia. We assume she was some monster

        but in fact she was *just a girl* before she became *just a girl in the world*, or

a girl who smashed through the world and commingled and was brought

        into orbit. This probably isn't

accurate. She was only the size of

        Mars. OK maybe a little bigger than Mars.

OK maybe she lied about her weight.

        OK maybe she lied about her ancient atmosphere

and supersonic winds and waves roiling across her magma ocean.

        There's not a girl alive

who doesn't know what I'm talking about. Theia had an atmosphere

        but it was like mostly sodium, it's not a big deal,

don't worry about it, I'm good, no you're fine, I'm fine.

        Is the moon even Theia anymore?

Is its surface still the rockbergs that formed it?

        Is that all that we'll let her be?

"Just A Girl" is the third song on No Doubt's 1995 album *Tragic Kingdom*.

The clear plastic phone revealed rainbow wires.

Gwen Stefani is a Libra.

This morning I gave up butter
and instantly lost my touch with eggs.
The olive oil overheated
and hot plumes popped in the air.

The child says a toy helicopter goes *up to the air in the sky.*

Sorry, I'm not home right now / I'm walking in a spiderweb

☽

Over tofu I declare   Percy Shelley's moon   was in Pisces,
        something I do not know
but of which I am sure
        because my guesses
about the nature of dark matter
        & energy   are invariably right.

(The heat death of the poet's ghost left me at an impasse.)

                (The ghost of his libido has a cosmic microwave background.)

To measure, poorly, the expansion of the universe, scientists look at how quickly
        something is moving

                                away from us   (mutability /

free love / multiple elopements / atheism / practice drowning / &c.)

        I still don't understand why he never learned to swim,   fish

as he was in his heart.   Look   how fast the universe is expanding.   How fast

        it was expanding   like   moon-clouds   *Streaking*

the darkness radiantly

☾

The scorpion stinger

        is a steak knife, a just-in-case

            they use when they can't rip

                grab tear their prey with their pincers. You said

          the scorpion is going to Vicarstown which is a place

      imaginary trains go *by the tree*

which was a cactus

☽

Elizabeth Bishop was born in the year of the metal pig, which sounds about right,

whereas I was born in the year of the wooden ox, &

we sit together on a shelf,   souvenirs   she picked up in her travels   our

Gemini moons   constructing endless

invisible metaphors.   Nan misspoke & said the coming year

would be good for oxen   & when she realized her mistake

tried to make me feel better   by txting *Chinese zodiac is culturally conservative*

so it thinks about futurity in similar ways like

it's time to lay low   *someone higher up will secretly help you out*   *don't travel*

& I am here for this excursus, scorpion queen

like when you told me the year of the dragon would pass me by

because *the dragon is a hegemonic shift*   *but oxen are slow*   *and stuck in the mud*

and don't care about hegemony   I almost bought a stone dragon at the festival & you said   *only a tourist would willingly bring a dragon into her home*

　　The scorpion child calls himself a dragon

procrastinating bedtime,　　he says he *wants to make the bed*　　which *is* made

　　　　& I don't know what he means

☾

So Coleridge flew his moon in Leo
    hence his insistence that he tell his story
much like the ancient mariner

    so the albatross was really a storm petrel
so I miscalculated Galileo's moon sign
    at four o'clock in the morning   not understanding the distinction

      between the Julian & Gregorian calendars

        a poem, like a birth chart, is a time capsule
        and every time capsule requires a miscalculation

and every miscalculation requires someone
who understands a story based on nothing can be true anyway

☾

the scorpion wakes up warm and milky

still heavy with sleep and welcoming

that scorpions glow in ultraviolet light

is perhaps because they are light collectors

and perhaps because they are giant eyes

a scorpion, though small, can see the stars

☾

III

 Serpentine

A tiger born on the first day of the week will have not one quality for the worst. A tiger born on the second day will be short-tempered. As the upper and lower waters divided, it is a day of contentiousness, but don't call her a *man-eater*, which is derogatory to all jungle cats, let alone those that actually devour men. A tiger born on the third day will be rich and/or promiscuous and/or able to escape from her habitat, as invasive species outgrow their landscaped lawns. In the days before the final frost, the scorpion child shakes out seeds from wildflowers and lacinato kale. A tiger born on the fourth day of the week will be wise, because of something about light, or heartbreak, or group text. A tiger born on the fifth day of the week will be kind, but have you ever met a kind tiger? Jar-stuck fist emoji, cucumber emoji, black heart emoji. A tiger born on the sixth day will be a seeker, averting her own extinction by competitive exclusion, by elevating a tacit assumption to a formal parameter in continuous time. A tiger born on the seventh day will die on the seventh day.

The time to extinction is basically infinite, is here already. Your nature is determined, not by the constellation of the day, but by the constellation of the hour. Somehow, your stripes never cross. The rabbis argued about whether astrology influenced the Hebrews, not whether astrology was real. All tigers are born under the influence of Mars, which is why they spill blood.

Abraham looked at his astrological map and saw he was not fit to have a son.

God told him to *emerge from his astrology*, and moved Jupiter to the East,

Jupiter, which sounds like the Hebrew word for justice.

God did this, I guess, for Abraham, and for his son.

A girl was going to the lake.

Ablet said to Shmuel, *a snake will bite her, and she will die*,

but she returned, with a snake cut in two in her Jansport backpack,

and Shmuel was like *WTF*, and she said

she had pretended to take bread from someone who didn't have bread so as not to

embarrass him for not having bread, and Shmuel was like, *whoa*.

The night before her wedding, Akiva's daughter

anointed herself with frankincense and myrrh and sprinkled lavender over the coverlet

of her bed and bathed in rosewater and healing salts.

She stuck her hairpin in a hole in the wall for safekeeping, thus impaling

the eye of the snake astrologers foretold would bite and kill her on her wedding day.

The time to extinction is basically infinite, I'm sure

the unlikely trio of tigers at the Denver aquarium could escape

if they were motivated. Like the lake girl, the Talmud tells us,

Akiva's daughter was also spared from the snake by virtue of charity,

in this case feeding the hungry, but I dunno.

If you cover a tiger's head, he cannot steal, despite his birth chart, unless he's sitting under a date tree, and looks up, and sees the fruits both ripe and dry and imagines his teeth sinking into that succulent flesh. In Guercino's *Amnon and Tamar*, the sister's belly is ripe like a fruit, and forsaken. She doesn't give a shit what her hair looks like and therein lies her beauty. When we passed it in the gallery, the scorpion child said he *found us*, which OK, it looks like us, but still. Amnon's shoulders, man, narrow but strong, and made for better things. How do you cover a tiger's head? A true maternal quandary. Knit him a hood of sugar and stars, sugar, which the scorpion child assumes must fall from the sky, like most sweet things. Guercino, a nickname, means *the squinter*, which might explain why the skin emits shards of light. His *Personification of Astrology* looks a little like me, OK she looks a lot like me, all waves and flesh and focus, that orange dress. If you cover a tiger's head, he's going to ask for a glass of milk. The artist's Aquarius sun rises in the branches, a tiger climbing after it, milk spilled despite his mother's best efforts. A date falls to the ground with a satisfying *plop*.

Aries looks like ovaries, is what I'm saying, the time to the full moon is infinite, is here already, if I can just hold on until Uranus slides into Taurus I'll be OK, I just know it, but instead I'm here in Gemini with Venus spilling glitter glue all over my tenth house of reputation.

My Virgo rising determines the spin of the wheel.
She puts the signs in their places.
She rearranges the furniture.

I mean if there is a snake here then where.
Like is it in the slide of Venus into Gemini, is it in some further sextile.

My Virgo rising is always misplacing me; it drives her fucking crazy.
The stripes of a tiger never cross.

A girl was going to the lake again, without her knives this time, in the light of the scorpion moon. Saturn, retrograde in Capricorn, rolled over Neptune, the planet of inspiration, hence these bad ideas. *Is the planet of productivity retrograding over the planet of inspiration a statement of poetics, is that a snake in the sand, shit did I leave my knives at home?* Saturn, despite its best efforts, has beautiful rings and is thus also a symbol of matrimony. Akiva's daughter thought long and hard about where to put her pin. She knew where the snake was hiding.

Like a tiger, the scorpion moon spills blood. The sun trines Saturn or sits sextile Neptune and the month unfolds. With the moon's fill and spill, the egg's release, her short stay. This is nothing that hasn't been said before. Nothing Akiva's daughter didn't know, or the girl at the lake. In astrology, each lunar cycle is an opening for motherhood, and each moment of birth is a determinate moment. The planets orbit the laboring body. The wave of contraction, the push and rest, the bleeding, bleeding out. We say *something is up with the planets* but we mean *the planets remember your mother in labor*. Akiva's daughter pauses by the wall. She has scrubbed her skin dry and is ready for bed. She has clothed herself in white and arranged her bed for the laying out, all petals and seeds, no blood to stain the sheets. She sets the hairpin down on her vanity, shakes her curls out, lies down on her back, places her hands on her heart and breathes. Sits up shaking, rushes to the wall, picks up the pin, and thrusts it into the animal's gleaming eye.

H.D.'s meticulous star charts live in a glass honeycomb, where they wait to tell me everything about modernism. I awake moments before the new moon in Taurus, ready. My antlers are always already a nest, are always already a fortress. I wash my teeth with peppermint, I put up water for tea, I wait for things to get rolling. I interrupt this mystical moment to email myself a few to-dos. It is a rainy morning and the moon is disappearing. I forgot about my boiling water. Black tea with peppermint. *Tea nana*. Don't get too political; this is an astrology poem. Don't think about the border to the holy land; don't think about the mothers. If we can just hold on until Uranus slips into Taurus, we'll all be fine. And that's a matter of days, I think. Maybe hours. The rabbis argued about whether astrology influenced the Hebrews, not whether astrology was real.

The scorpion child says the moon *gets smaller and smaller*, asks if you can talk about the moon again, and together you spin out a story about alligators hosting a moon party, about stingrays using their tails to knit socks, about sharks putting on shoes and walking over the water, is every story a call for messiah, is every story a plea for redemption. Chani Nicholas invokes the fixed star Algol as Medusa's blinking eye which, conjunct the invisible moon, both is and is not the female body. In seminar we read Catherine as in labor and Heathcliff as the father, thus the former's death in premature childbirth seven months after the arrival of the latter, and hence the latter's statement—"I love *my* murderer—but *yours*! How can I?"—commonly read as self-indictment but perhaps in fact a justification for ultimately mistreating the little girl of whom Catherine will be delivered, albeit unsafely, a few hours later. That little girl is a Pisces on the cusp of Aries, Emily Brontë had the moon in Cancer, where it's at home, as she usually was. New moon sunrise yellows the trees. Akiva's daughter wakes and dresses, not pausing to reconsider her options.

Ablet said to Shmuel, a snake will bite her, and she will die, do you think we should tell her, I mean she's going to go to the lake in either case, *amiright*, it's written in the stars, and anyway we just got comfortable, and the girl kept walking, she walked all the way down to the lake, and she took off her headscarf, revealing a head of snakes, and she shook them out and OK, maybe you're scared but watch her, watch the split tongues swinging around her tan shoulders, listen, listen to the hissing.

A tiger bats at a stone lazily with her paw.

It is serpentine breccia, not unlike a snake or something found on the moon.

Her eyes blink like binary stars.

She gets up. She stretches.

It is late evening. It is quiet.

She circles the house.

She sees a snake skulking, wonders

        for a moment if it is a tiger snake, which would be funny,

but probably it isn't.

The snake lies in wait, listening with its invisible ears, listening through the wall.

A pin spikes through the wall, just missing its eye.

I can fix that, thinks the tiger.

IV

Other

People's

Scorpions

after H.D.

[1]

At the sugar cereal restaurant   Sarah Allison

                                        said in regards to babies as scorpions

but scorpions are so hard,   and babies are so   *soft*

and also because   of how they are

and she cupped her hands   while my child drank strawberry milk

and her sons picked out the marshmallows   to show how a baby curls up

                        when it rolls over   reaching for your arm

or ear   or breast   and recently someone said   *there is no such thing*

as other people's children   which was the sweetest lie   I had heard   in a long time

[2]

at the border   (write it(the new Eve

    at the border the new Eve steps over the threshold

her moon, like mine   is in Gemini,

        which is why she talks to snakes

Sarah Allison's moon   is in Aries   hence her desire to make
         hard things   her own   *Aries, the Ram;*

                                              time, time for you to begin a new spiral

Aries   looks like ovaries   that dip&twist

[4]

Uranus is in Taurus & so

                     I have come to H.D. to learn astrology

relating, I suppose, to that combination of skepticism & obsession

      a sort of rational pursuit of the irrational   that defines   if we're being honest

modernism for me

                    in her astrology notebook she writes

3 decades for each Sign of Zodiac.
12 Signs = 36 decades.
72 Names of God + attributes.
72 Angels' Names - 72 degrees.
    72 Degrees = 72 Names.
    ~~*5circles*~~ divisions, of days, each year.

[5]

Other people's children have   one name, maybe two

but your own soft scorpion   & his many names   the one he gives

himself when he is playing stingray,   the one he gives   the sea turtle,

which stretches its rubber   what do we want to call them   fins

feet   paddles   *I want no shoes just   socks I mean   no socks*

just shoes   But who   my mother wants to know   her Capricorn moon

loose   who   who   whom   Who takes the child   off the breast

who follows the command   and I   the phone

my scorpion   tired at the art gallery   motherhood is a constant interruption

but we are talking about motherhood

interrupted

[6]

*Séphira_*   *plural,*   *Sephiroth_*   i.e. the ways in which the infinite

        relates to the finite   an old friend   who was probably an Aquarius

tried to get me hooked   on Kabbalah but it promises

        a better world   which is not this world   wherefore this list

of angels & degrees   why   is the name *Moti*   in here, Moti, the mouse

        in your book?   I say I have been *teaching myself astrology for a poetry project*

but is any of that   quite right?   I have been searching for Moti

        the mitzvah mouse in H.D.'s 1960 astrology notebook

but what   am I really trying to find   I mean who moved

                                                    my cheese?

[7]

Pearls are called *moti* in India.

In astrology, they might give strength to the moon, or support a strong moon, so
    if you believe in tokens and things like that

you could wear one if you wanted
    we have been separating families
our nation has been separating families
    parents from children and then children from their siblings
and the news is moving so fast   so I need to put it in a poem
    so that I am seeing it,   so that I am slowing down
the news and seeing it again this is no pearl   of wisdom

    but can a poem be a token
         can a poem be something hard inside that is coming to a shine
I want to hold each child in my arms during this hardening

    all scorpions glow   in the dark

[8]

What does it mean   to say each sign has decades   does it mean   my birth

on the last day of Taurus   explains why I'm   the worst

of both worlds?   H.D.'s later psychoanalyst Erich   Heydt

prompted H.D.'s memoir   of her relationship with Ezra Pound.

Regarding the placement of Uranus in Heydt's chart,

H.D. wrote,

This might make for immense, almost super-natural
drive and power. Herschel is the so-called X-ray planet, governing new ideas, all the
dangerous and healing and newly discouvered [sic] *and not yet discouvered*
"rays", radium and the like.

In her star charts, H.D. refers to her daughter, sometimes as *The Fire Girl*,

sometimes as *Pup*.

There is a mouse   or a cat

    creeping across a conception chart   H.D. had drawn up

    for Kenneth Macpherson (Kex)   who was ~~probably~~ her lover

      as well as collaborator   not to mention important   to the history

of film and who   is "The New Ram"   whose chart the archivists

    have not identified?   It isn't Ezra Pound, that scorpion

problem,   his birth time unknown,   at least to H.D., who suspected

    he had Capricorn rising. It isn't   T. S. Eliot, fellow Gemini moon,

which explains the mermaids singing, nor   D. H. Lawrence nor Sigmund Freud so who?

[10]

Who is the new ram & do I prefer   to find out?   Aries   looks like ovaries

        is all I'm saying   it holds the stars   of the spring equinox

    its horn, blown, proclaims the new year

                                        shofar   *so good*

        the first sign   of the zodiac   ram-horned Zeus   ram-headed god

of the source   of the Nile

[11]

probably not her stillborn daughter
        nor yet the messiah (we'd have known by now)
The New Ram has the sun in Taurus
       and both Mars and the moon in Virgo   if I'm reading things right

The deeper we get into the day   farther away   miles

    from the last time I checked the news   the easier it is not to consider

to unconsider the night terrors from which   very soft scorpions   refuse to wake

    their hands flailing to hold your hand   in the dark

                    in the dark in which they glow

so you can find them

[13]

When the mother comes to your gates, her heart   wrapped in linens   in her arms
        & smelling of dirt   and lilies,
                                let her in.

she brings the Book of Life, obviously.

NEW HAVEN
JUNE 20, 2018

notes

&

acknowledgments

When I mention Chani Nicholas, I most often refer to her online courses, *Workshop for the New Moon in Aries* (http://**www.chaninicholas.com**, April 2018), *Workshop for the New Moon in Taurus* (http://**www.chaninicholas.com**, May 2018), and *Your Moon: Understanding the moon in your chart* (http://**www.chaninicholas.com**), all of which were foundational to my research for, and infuse, this project. My understanding of astrology is also informed by Nicholas's social media presence, newsletters, and so forth. The reference to "The Voluptuous Witch" ([According to Emily aka *The Voluptuous Witch*]) is to Emily Heather Price's online course *Lucky Witch: a Jupiter in Sagittarius Guide* (www. thevoluptuouswitch.com, November 2018). I was reading a lot of articles about science and outer space when I wrote this book, mostly in *New Scientist*. I also sometimes wrote in response to prompts in Kelli Russell Agodon and Martha Silano's *The Daily Poet* (Kingston, WA: Two Sylvias Press, 2013). When researching the birth charts of historical figures and people I don't know, I used online resources including Astrotheme (http://www.astrotheme.com) and Astro Databank (http://www.astro.com/astro-databank/).

I *slippage*

[Over shishito peppers] includes fragments from a letter from Silvia Dobson to H.D. ("My dear Cat") dated "May 4th Woodhall. Shipbourne. Tonbridge. Kent," H.D. Papers, Yale Collection of American Literature, Beinecke Rare Book and Manuscript Library. The lines "I myself am hell; / nobody's here—" are from Robert Lowell's "Skunk Hour." The line by Barthes is from "Astrology" in *Mythologies*, translated by Richard Howard and Annette Lavers (New York: Hill and Wang, 2012), 188. I also include a line from H.D.'s *The Gift: The Complete Text*, edited by Jane Augustine (Gainesville: University Press of Florida, 1998), 79. Rebecca Colesworthy discusses this passage in context in *Returning the Gift: Modernism and the Thought of Exchange* (New York: Oxford University Press, 2018), 232.

[Waxing crescent moon in Sagittarius a million stock photos of the moon] concludes with a line from one of H.D.'s letters quoted in H.D., *Trilogy*, edited by Aliki Barnstone (New York: New Directions, 1998), 79.

II *lunar fragments for the scorpion child*

[The Sun Is a Bomb Cyclone] includes fragments from Samuel Taylor Coleridge's "Frost at Midnight"; [Over tofu I declare] concludes with a fragment from Percy Bysshe Shelley's "Mutability."

Several of these fragments first appeared in journals, sometimes in earlier forms. [The night of the mid-autumn festival] and [The moon is in Taurus] first appeared in *Moonchild Magazine*. [This is a lunar fragment], [I had a strange Yom Kippur], [At the Vermeer exhibit], [On Nan's birthday], and [The scorpion stinger] first appeared in *TIMBER*. [The sun is a bomb cyclone] first appeared in *Occulum*. [I am skimming the edges] first appeared in *Pithead Chapel*. [Sheera's moon is in Libra], [I want to write a confessional poem], and [A child makes a zoographia of open things] first appeared in *Dream Pop*. [Four centuries ago this month] first appeared in *Bombus Press*. I am grateful to the editors of these publications for their support of the project.

[the scorpion wakes up warm and milky] mentions the idea that scorpions might be giant eyes. For more on this, see Douglas D. Gaffin, Lloyd A. Bumm, Matthew S. Taylor, Nataliya V. Popokina, and Shivani Mann, "Scorpion fluorescence and reaction to light," *Animal Behavior* 83, no. 2 (February 2012): 429–36.

III *serpentine*

This section plays with material from the Talmud, specifically tractate Shabbat, folio 156. [The scorpion child says the moon gets *smaller and smaller*] includes a line from Emily Brontë's *Wuthering Heights*. Some of the language about extinction in this section manipulates phrases from the following article: Nathaniel J. Dominy and Justin D. Yeakel, "*Frankenstein* and the Horrors of Competitive Exclusion," *BioScience* 67, no. 2 (February 2017): 107–10.

IV *other people's scorpions*

This serial poem first appeared as an online chapbook from *Moonchaps* (*Moonchild Magazine*), edited, designed, and published by Nadia Gerassimenko, to whom I am grateful. The lines "this is the new Eve" and "she brings the Book of Life, obviously" come from H.D.'s "Tribute to the Angels." The lines "Aries, the Ram; / time, time for you to begin a new spiral" come from H.D.'s *The Walls Do Not Fall*. I am indebted to Aliki Barnstone's excellent "Readers' Notes" on the work, as well. H.D., *Trilogy*, edited by Aliki Barnstone (New York: New Directions, 1998), 101, 30, 173–201.

I wrote this poem in the Beinecke Rare Book and Manuscript Library surrounded by H.D.'s astrology papers while my mother entertained my son in New Haven. The quoted fragments in [4] and [6] are from [Astrology: notes 1960]. The quoted material in [8] is from [Horoscope reading for Erich Heydt]. H.D. refers to her daughter, Frances Perdita (Aldington) Macpherson Schaffner, as "The Fire Girl" in a star chart drawn on a sheet of notebook paper [Astrology: horoscopes 1953–59]. Perdita is referred to as "Pup" in a book of star charts executed for H.D. by Silvia Dobson. I also refer to this book in [9] through [11]. H.D. Papers, Yale Collection of American Literature, Beinecke Rare Book and Manuscript Library.

☾

I am grateful to my editor, Rebecca Colesworthy, who saw a handful of these poems and got the whole picture, who helped this book come into being with rigor and grace, who shares my commitments to both H.D. and '90s music, and who let me dish about her chart in the second poem. I am grateful to the two anonymous peer reviewers whose feedback helped me sharpen and streamline the manuscript, to Jenn Bennett-Genthner for her clarifying copyedits, and to the team at SUNY Press for making this book come to life. Thanks to Aimee Harrison for her exacting attention to layout and design, and to Zoe Norvell for such a fun yet scorpionic cover. Séan Richardson shared his archival images with me before I was able to travel to New Haven myself, Rebecca Aldi and colleagues were tremendously helpful during my research trip to the Beinecke Rare Book and Manuscript

Library, and Sierra Shaffer, Sarah Ehlers, and Jason and Jonah Berger introduced me to New Haven pizza. To my poetry teachers—especially Jane Hilberry, who taught me to honor my obsessions, and Lorna Goodison, who taught me to embrace the life of the non-poet— thank you. This collection, like all the work I do, comes out of and documents an ongoing conversation with Nan Z. Da about literature and womanhood and culture and how to live and what to do. Her text messages while I was writing this book often struck upon Chinese astrology and other cultural formations as the perfect media for expressing complicated identities in an accelerated way; now that her texts are in the book, she is texting you, too. Other friendly interlocutors in these poems, both named and unnamed, include Rebecca Ariel Porte, Chet Lisiecki, Anahid Nersessian, Sierra Shaffer, Sheera Talpaz, McCormick Templeman, and Sarah Allison. [The scorpion children play dragon and unicorn] and [Four centuries ago this month] are for Julia Michie Bruckner. Thanks to my birth family—Rob, Andrea, and Jed—who create constellations where before there was only the sky. The best husband in the universe, Moshe Kornfeld, encouraged me to write this book in all the most Virgo ways possible; I wouldn't have written it if not for him. And to the scorpion child, who energized this book with his insight, sweetness, and early words: I love you from the shoes and socks to the moon and stars, and all the way back.

Rachel Feder is an assistant
professor of English and literary arts
at the University of Denver. Her previous
publications include a poetry chapbook, *Words With Friends* (2014), a book-length serial
poem, *Bad Romanticisms* (2018), and a work of experimental literary criticism, *Harvester
of Hearts: Motherhood under the Sign of* Frankenstein (2018).